Extinct Giants

Hawys Morgan

Explorer Challenge

Find out which animal
had teeth like these ...

OXFORD

UNIVERSITY PRESS

Contents

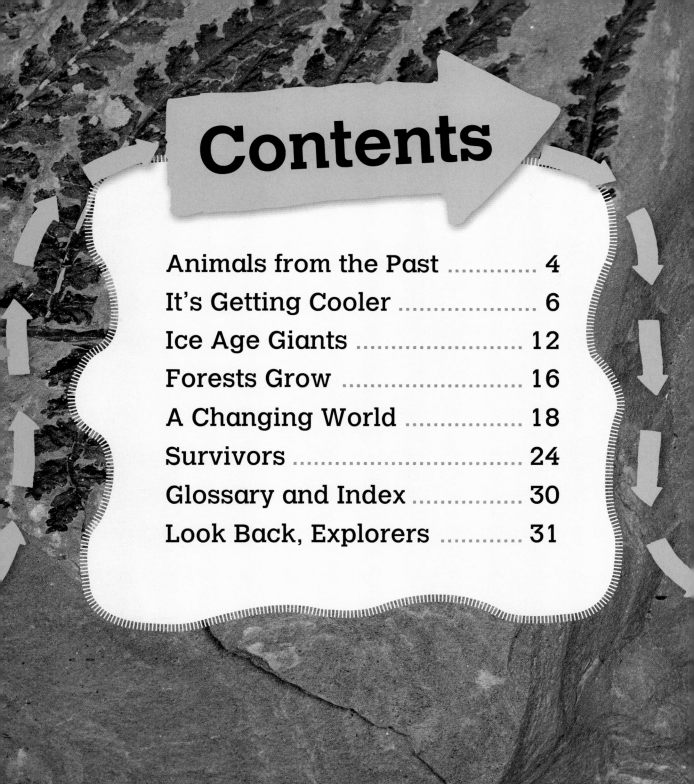

Animals from the Past

There are many amazing animals living on planet Earth,
from tiny frogs to huge elephants.
But some animals are extinct.

Extinct animals were alive in the past, but they are not alive today. An extinct animal will never be seen alive again.

Can you spot any extinct animals on these pages?

It's Getting Cooler

Over 65 million years ago, the Earth was much hotter than it is today. Then volcanoes erupted over many years. A big **asteroid** might have smashed into the Earth.

Some scientists think that clouds of ash and dust blocked out the sunlight.

The Earth became cooler over millions of years. As it cooled down, many animals became extinct.

The megalodon (*say* meg-a-loa-don) lived millions of years ago.

megalodon jaw

Fossils and bones help scientists find out what extinct animals looked like and how they lived.

It was the largest shark ever to have existed. Some megalodons were about 14 metres (m) long. They ate large whales.

1.8m

great white shark

4.5m

megalodon

14m

The titanoboa (*say* tigh-tan-a-boa-a) was the largest snake that ever lived. It was about 13 metres long. It was so big it could have eaten a crocodile.

1.8m

13m

titanoboa

boa constrictor

3m

This was the biggest rat that ever lived! It was about three metres long and weighed around 1000 kilograms. That's about as heavy as two polar bears!

3m

25 centimetres (cm)

1.8m

giant rat

guinea pig

Ice Age Giants

When the Earth gets very cold, it is called an **Ice Age**. Many Ice Age animals had thick fur to keep out the cold.

woolly mammoth

smilodon

Smilodons (*say* smile-oa-dons) had big teeth. Some of their teeth were nearly three times bigger than a tiger's teeth! They ate young woolly mammoths.

smilodon

20cm

7cm

tiger

Scientists know a lot about woolly mammoths because whole animals have been found frozen in ice. Scientists have also looked at the mammoths' frozen **dung**! The dung shows that mammoths ate grass, moss and flowers.

1.8m

woolly mammoth

3.3m

African elephant

3.3m

Glyptodons (*say* glip-toa-dons) looked like giant armadillos. Some were about three metres long. They had thick bony shells, and big heavy tails.

1.8m

glyptodon

armadillo

75cm

3m

Forests Grow

About 11000 years ago, the Earth got warmer. Forests began to grow in places where there used to be grass. Some scientists think not all animals could find enough grass to eat.

Cave paintings show people hunting animals. People hunted animals for food. They used animal skins to make clothes.

Some animals may have become extinct because of hunting and because there wasn't enough food for them.

Can you tell what animals are in the cave painting?

A Changing World

Have you ever heard someone say, "As dead as a dodo"? It means completely dead. Dodos are birds that are extinct now. They became extinct about 350 years ago.

Dodos couldn't fly and laid their eggs on the ground. When sailors arrived on the dodos' island they had animals like dogs, cats and rats with them. The animals were able to eat the dodo eggs. Sailors also hunted the dodos.

1.8m

1m

40cm

chicken   dodo

Steller's sea cows were giants of the sea. They were ten metres long. Some may have weighed about 11000 kilograms. That's twice as heavy as an elephant!

They didn't have any teeth and ate seaweed. They often floated on top of the sea. This made it easier for humans to hunt them, so Steller's sea cows became extinct.

1.8m

1.5m

harbour seal

Steller's sea cow

10m

Elephant birds were the largest birds that ever lived. They lived on the island of Madagascar.

Elephant birds were over three metres tall. One elephant bird egg was bigger than 150 chicken's eggs!

We aren't sure why these birds became extinct, but we know that people hunted them. The elephant birds couldn't fly so maybe it was difficult for them to escape.

elephant bird

chicken

1.8m

3m

40cm

Survivors

Not all animals become extinct. Some animals today are closely related to animals from millions of years ago.

This is a nautilus. It has nearly 100 tentacles.

The nautilus is related to a similar sea animal that lived about 400 million years ago. This is the sea animal's fossil.

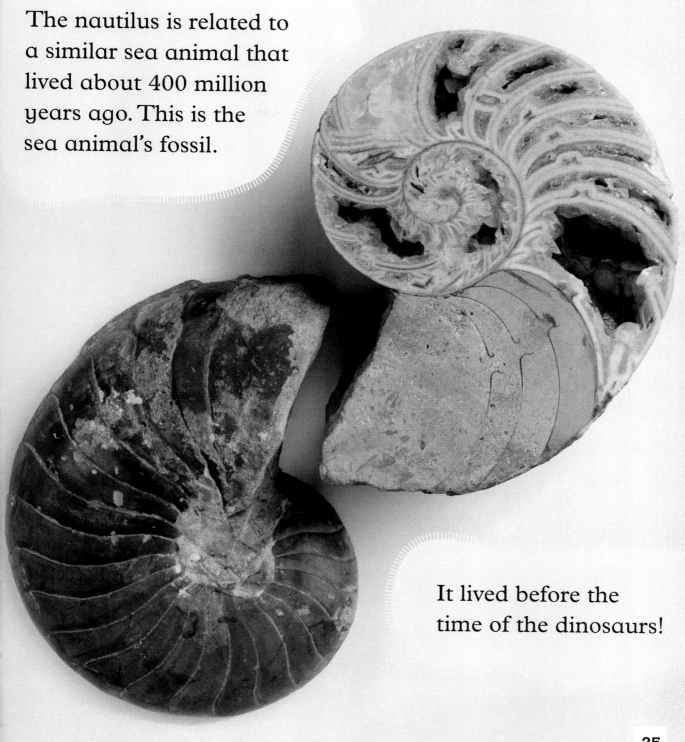

It lived before the time of the dinosaurs!

A horseshoe crab has ten legs under its shell. It looks a bit like a crab, but it's more closely related to a scorpion or a spider.

The horseshoe crabs alive today are very similar to those that lived over 400 million years ago.

Pelicans have the longest beak of any living bird. They have a soft pouch under their beaks where they catch their food.

Pelicans are very like birds that lived about 30 million years ago.

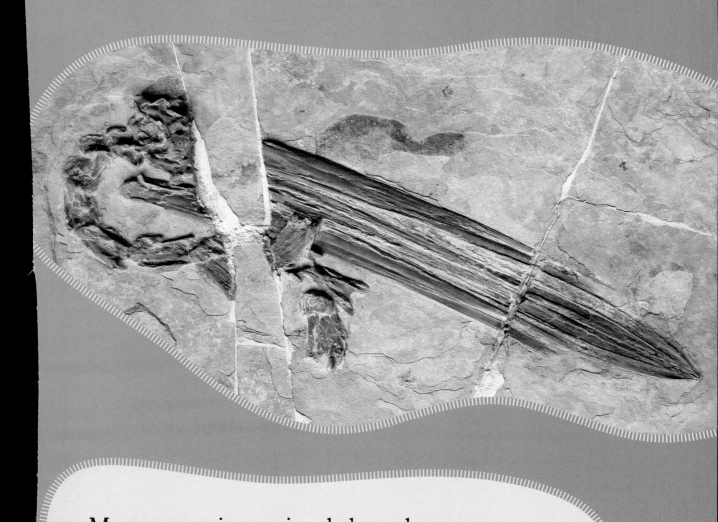

Many amazing animals have become extinct. If you could bring an extinct animal back to life, which one would you choose?

Glossary

asteroid: a rock that travels through space

dung: solid droppings from animals

extinct animals: animals that can never be seen alive again

fossils: the shapes of plants or animals that have turned into rock

Index

Look Back, Explorers

How large was the titanoboa?

What did smilodons eat?

Look back at pages 16–17.
Imagine you are meeting the people
who lived at that time. What questions
would you ask them?

Steller's sea cows were 'giants
of the sea'. Look at pages 20–21.
How would you describe them?

How are the woolly mammoth and
African elephant on page14 similar?

Did you find out
which animal had
teeth like these?

What's Next, Explorers?

Now you know about these extinct giants, read about what happens when Wilf and Wilma spot a very old bone ...

A **Mammoth** Task

Series created by Roderick Hunt and Alex Brychta

OXFORD

Explorer Challenge
for *A Mammoth Task*

Find out what Mum picks up by the cliffs ...